# THIS BOOK BELONGS TO:

# TABLE OF CONTENTS

**HI, KIDS!** I'm Dash Derby, and I'll be your guide through the daring world of Pinewood Derby racing. Use this workbook along with the book *Getting Starting in Pinewood Derby* to learn the basics of building a Derby car. Check out all the cool ideas and pick a few to make your car look awesome! Then, work through the set-up sections and record your progress along the way. After all the hard work is done, you can glue pictures of your speedy car right into this book and record your memories of the race so you'll never forget. Stick with me and these guides, and you'll have an awesome car built in no time. Let's get started!

### Dash's Rules for
## Derby Adventurers

1. Have **FUN!**

2. Don't wait until the last minute to get started.

3. If you get tired, stop.

4. Don't let your parents take over—this is your project.

5. The derby isn't about winning—it's about having fun and learning new skills along the way!

## Materials & Tool List...

- ☐ Pinewood Derby kit
- ☐ Pencil
- ☐ Ruler
- ☐ Wood clamps
- ☐ Coping saw
- ☐ Sandpaper (100 grit)
- ☐ Sandpaper (150 grit)
- ☐ Painter's masking tape
- ☐ Glue Stick
- ☐ Elbow grease

> The toughest part of making a car is choosing the design.

**1** **Get the pattern ready.**
Cut out the pattern. Put glue on the pattern.

**2** **Put the pattern on the block.**
Line up the block on the paper.

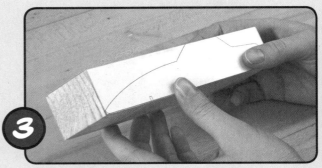

**3** **Cut out the car.**
Use a coping saw to cut out the car.

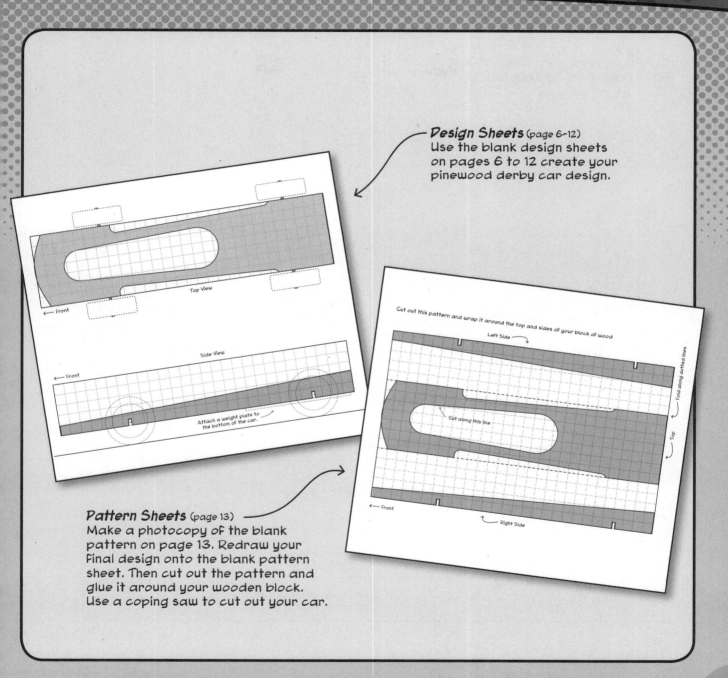

**Design Sheets** (page 6-12)
Use the blank design sheets on pages 6 to 12 create your pinewood derby car design.

**Pattern Sheets** (page 13)
Make a photocopy of the blank pattern on page 13. Redraw your final design onto the blank pattern sheet. Then cut out the pattern and glue it around your wooden block. Use a coping saw to cut out your car.

Top View

← Front

Side View

← Front

Attach a weight plate to the bottom of the car.

Cut out this pattern and wrap it around the top and sides of your block of wood

Left Side →

Cut along this line

Fold along dotted lines

Top

← Front

Right Side

# MY DESIGNS

Use these blank car blocks to draw
some ideas for car designs.

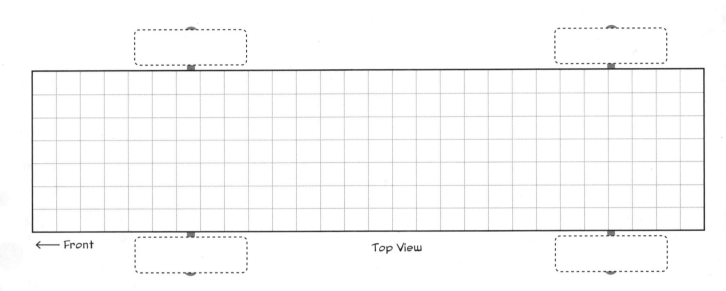

← Front

Top View

← Front

Side View

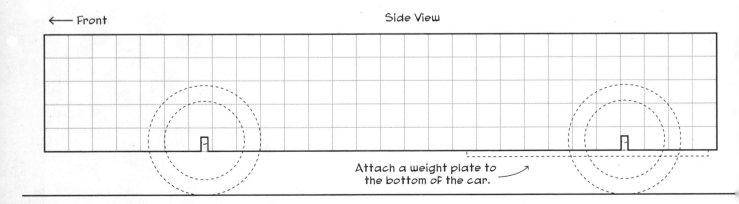

Attach a weight plate to
the bottom of the car.

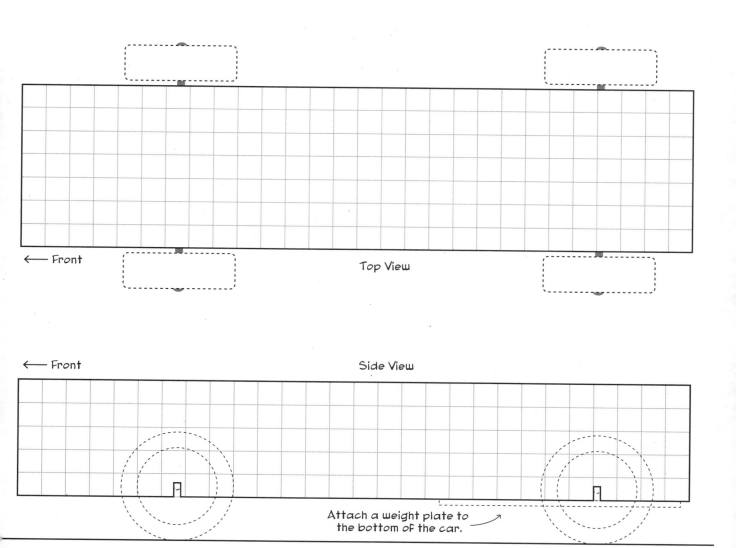

← Front            Top View

← Front            Side View

Attach a weight plate to the bottom of the car.

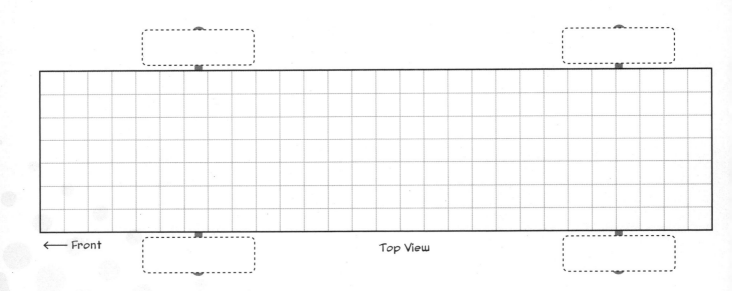

← Front · Top View

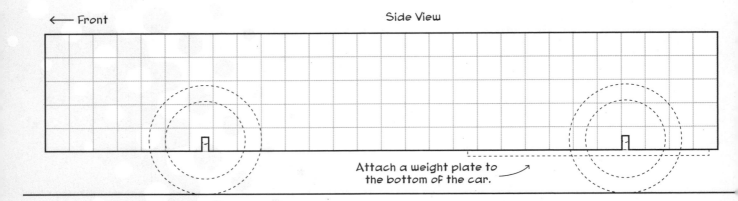

← Front · Side View

Attach a weight plate to the bottom of the car.

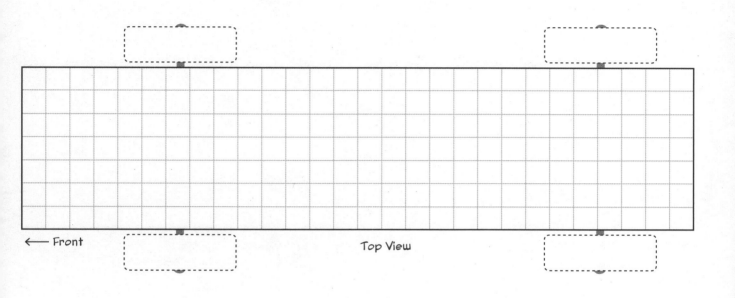

← Front          Top View

← Front          Side View

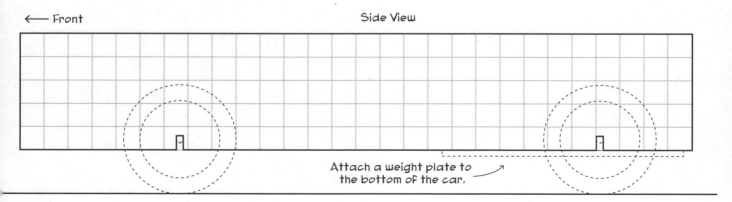

Attach a weight plate to the bottom of the car.

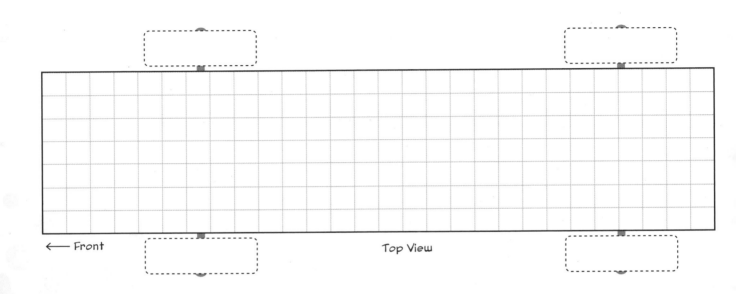

← Front                                    Top View

← Front                                    Side View

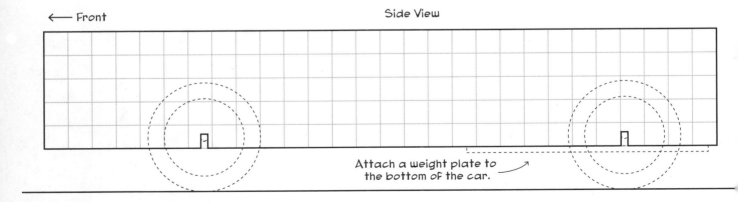

Attach a weight plate to
the bottom of the car.

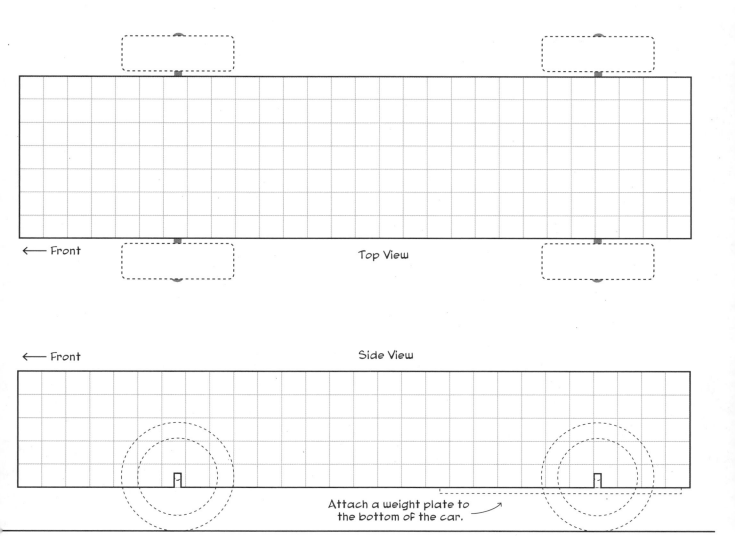

← Front          Top View

← Front          Side View

Attach a weight plate to
the bottom of the car.

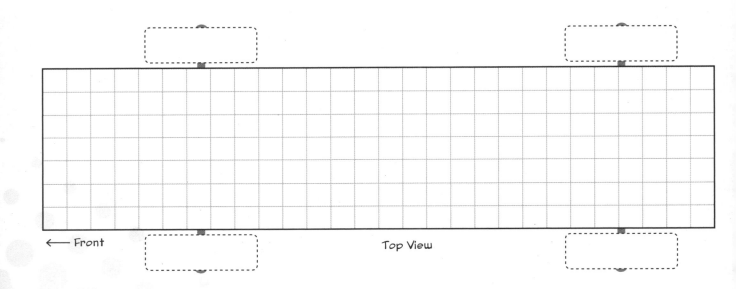

← Front

Top View

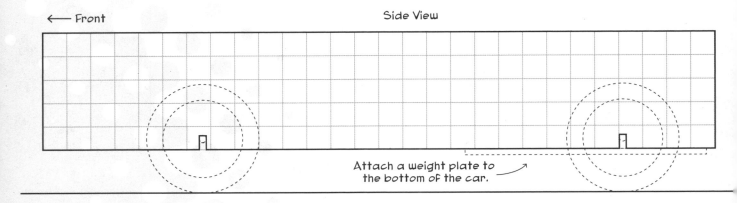

← Front

Side View

Attach a weight plate to the bottom of the car.

Cut out this pattern and wrap it around
the top and sides of your block of wood.

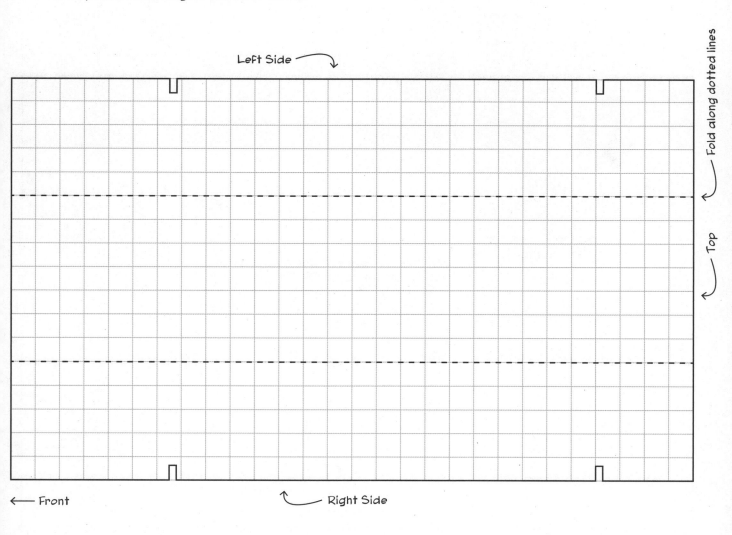

Left Side

Fold along dotted lines

Top

Front

Right Side

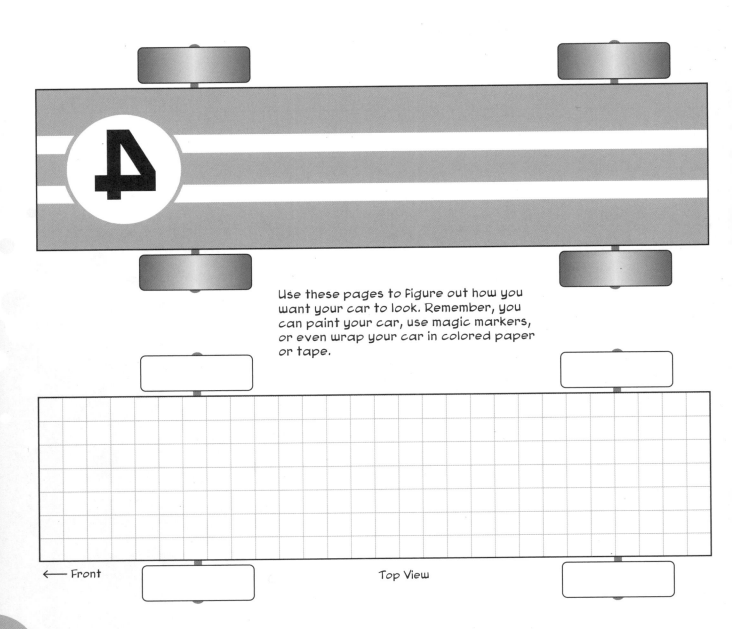

Use these pages to figure out how you want your car to look. Remember, you can paint your car, use magic markers, or even wrap your car in colored paper or tape.

← Front

Top View

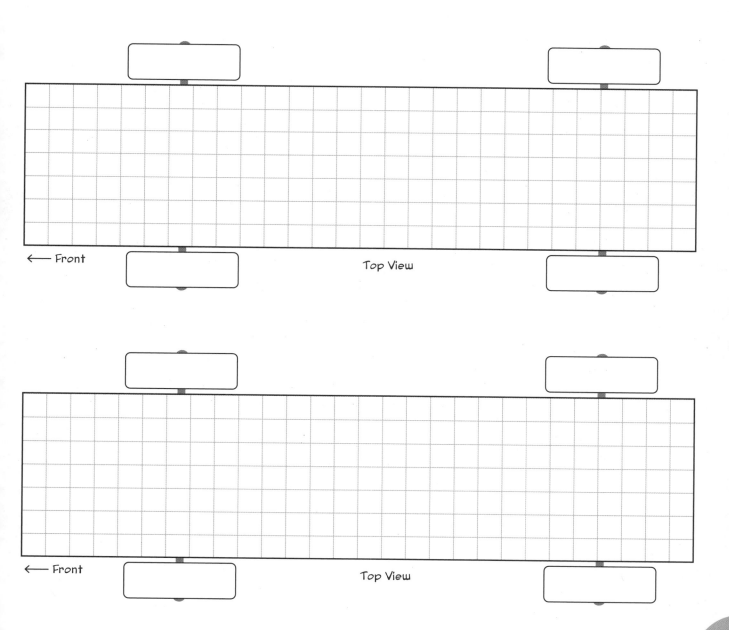

←— Front             Top View

←— Front             Top View

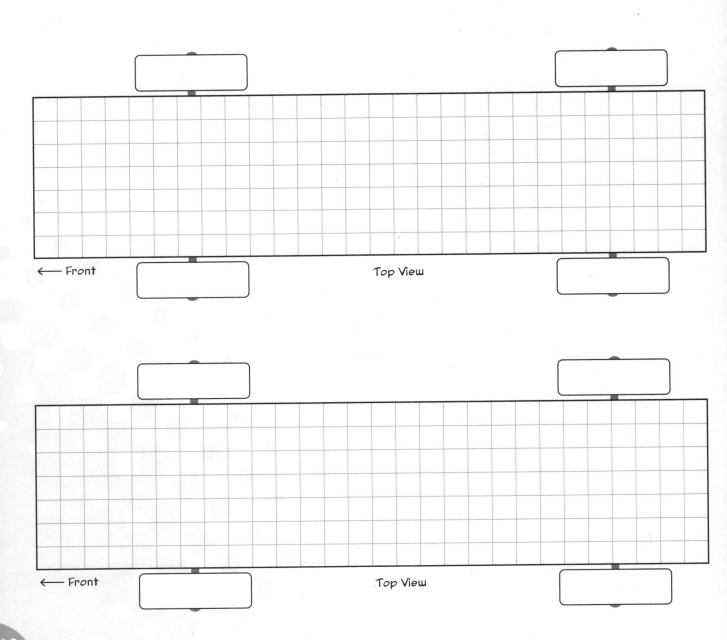

← Front

Top View

← Front

Top View

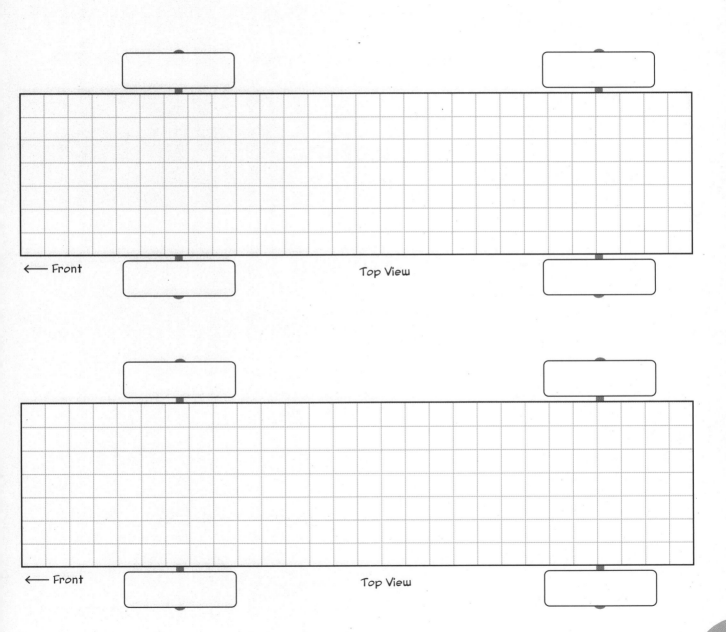

← Front     Top View

← Front     Top View

# PAINTING IDEAS

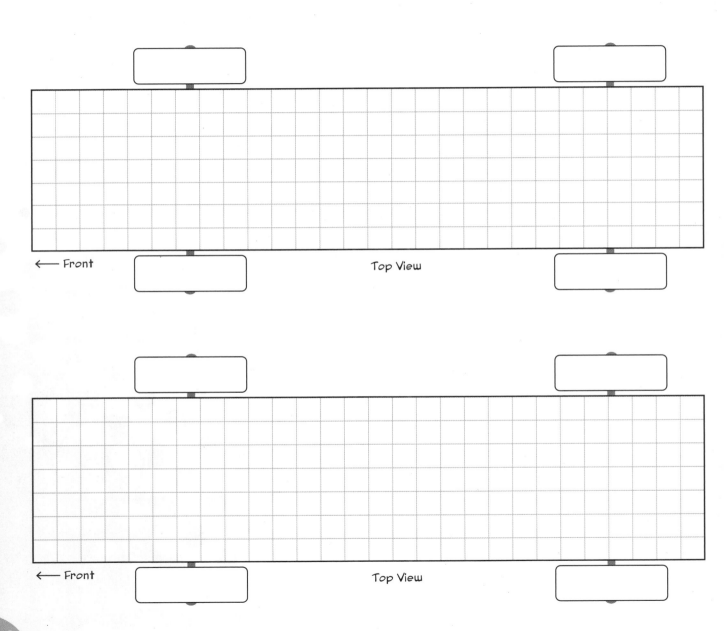

← Front                    Top View

← Front                    Top View

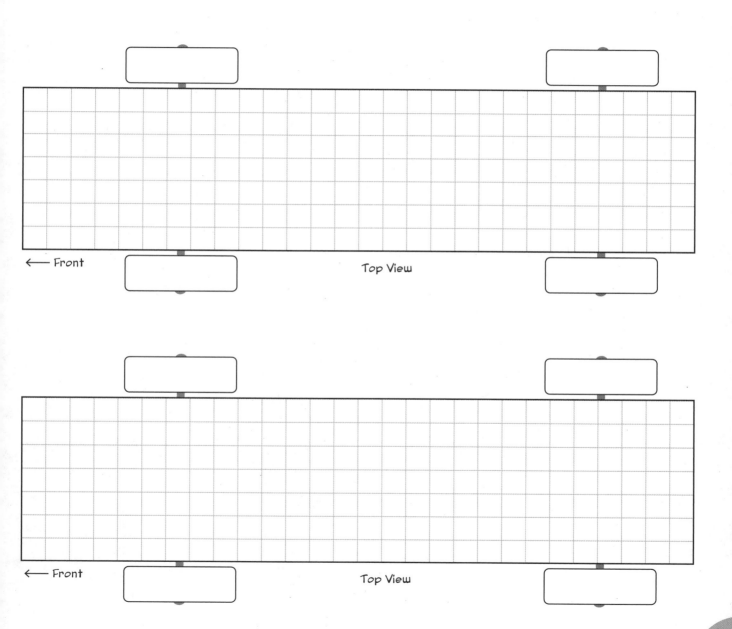

← Front       Top View

← Front       Top View

# EXTRA DETAILS

**Design Elements**
Use these basic elements to
start your awesome design!

0 1 2 3 4
5 6 7 8 9

2 4 3

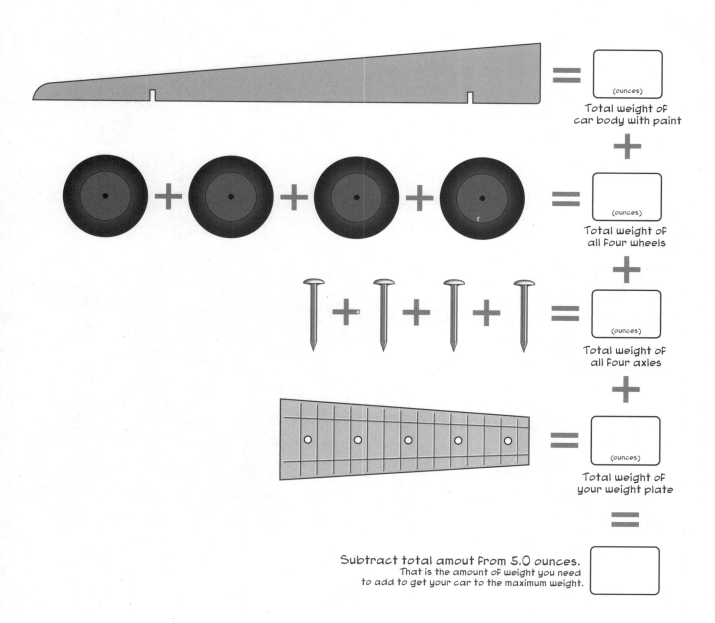

= (ounces)
Total weight of
car body with paint

+

= (ounces)
Total weight of
all four wheels

+

= (ounces)
Total weight of
all four axles

+

= (ounces)
Total weight of
your weight plate

=

Subtract total amout from 5.0 ounces.
That is the amount of weight you need
to add to get your car to the maximum weight.

# TEST RUN LOGS

Set up the board so it has an angle to it. Tape a straight path down the board and put something soft at the bottom to cushion the car. Put the car at the top and see what happens!

*Graphite can be messy! It takes a gentle touch—just like adjusting your car's steering.*

## Materials & Tool List...

- ☐ Table leaf or long, flat board
- ☐ Place mat or other soft, thick cloth
- ☐ Masking or painter's tape
- ☐ Level
- ☐ Permanent marker
- ☐ Small flat screwdriver
- ☐ Hammer
- ☐ Graphite

**If your car curves left:**
Rotate your steering axle counter-clockwise 45°. See the top illustration on the next page.

**If your car goes straight down the middle:**
Don't touch a thing! You're ready to go!

**If your car curves right:**
Rotate your steering axle clockwise 45°. See the bottom illustration on the next page.

If your car curves left...

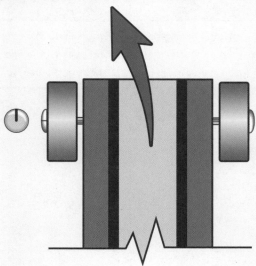

...Rotate the axle counter-clockwise 45°. This tilts the axle bend forward.

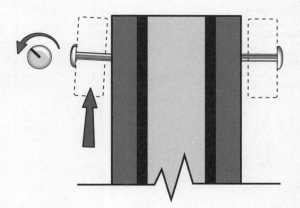

If your car curves right...

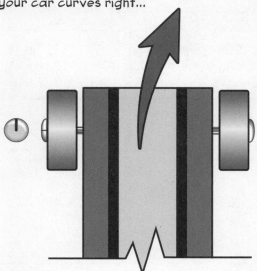

...Rotate the axle clockwise 45°. This tilts the axle bend backward.

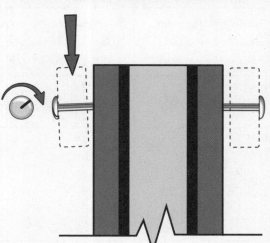

## Car Alignment Tests

| Test Run #1 | Test Run #2 | Test Run #3 | Test Run #4 |
|---|---|---|---|
| ☐ Car pulls to the right<br>☐ Car pulls to the left<br>☐ Stays in the center | ☐ Car pulls to the right<br>☐ Car pulls to the left<br>☐ Stays in the center | ☐ Car pulls to the right<br>☐ Car pulls to the left<br>☐ Stays in the center | ☐ Car pulls to the right<br>☐ Car pulls to the left<br>☐ Stays in the center |
| Axle Angle:<br>Record the angle of your axle here ➔ | Axle Angle: | Axle Angle: | Axle Angle: |
| Notes: | Notes: | Notes: | Notes: |

## Car Alignment Tests

| Test Run #5 | Test Run #6 | Test Run #7 | Test Run #8 |
|---|---|---|---|
| ☐ Car pulls to the right<br>☐ Car pulls to the left<br>☐ Stays in the center | ☐ Car pulls to the right<br>☐ Car pulls to the left<br>☐ Stays in the center | ☐ Car pulls to the right<br>☐ Car pulls to the left<br>☐ Stays in the center | ☐ Car pulls to the right<br>☐ Car pulls to the left<br>☐ Stays in the center |
| Axle Angle: | Axle Angle: | Axle Angle: | Axle Angle: |
| Notes: | Notes: | Notes: | Notes: |

## Car Alignment Tests

| Test Run #9 | Test Run #10 | Test Run #11 | Test Run #12 |
|---|---|---|---|
| ☐ Car pulls to the right<br>☐ Car pulls to the left<br>☐ Stays in the center | ☐ Car pulls to the right<br>☐ Car pulls to the left<br>☐ Stays in the center | ☐ Car pulls to the right<br>☐ Car pulls to the left<br>☐ Stays in the center | ☐ Car pulls to the right<br>☐ Car pulls to the left<br>☐ Stays in the center |
| Axle Angle: ◯<br>Record the angle of your axle here → | Axle Angle: ◯ | Axle Angle: ◯ | Axle Angle: ◯ |
| Notes: | Notes: | Notes: | Notes: |

## TIP BREAKING IN THE WHEELS

One of the best tips for making your car run smoothly is breaking in the wheels. The easiest way to do this is to spin the wheels with your finger. As you spin each wheel, the graphite will work into the nooks and crannies and make everything smooth and polished. The smoother and more polished the axle is, the faster your car will go! It's a good idea to watch a TV show or movie while you do this, because you can spend 15 minutes or so per wheel if you want. While you spin the wheels, be careful not to bump the alignment too much. You'll probably need to do another test run afterward to make sure everything is lined up, but you don't want to do any damage while you're breaking in the wheels. Spin carefully!

## What to Bring to the race

- [ ] Small screwdriver
- [ ] Extra split shot
- [ ] Extra graphite or lube
- [ ] Super glue
- [ ] Tape
- [ ] Camera or video camera
- [ ] Money for snacks
- [ ] This book and a pen to record your race times

**Weigh-in:** When you get to the race, you'll have to weigh your car to prove that it weighs the correct five ounces. Here's a method to practice at home. Put your scale on the table and carefully place the car on the scale. It is important to put the car on the scale upside down—that way, your car can't roll off and mess up your wheel alignment. Add small weights to the scale until it reads exactly 5.0 ounces. Then, add those weights to the car. If you practice this, when you show up at weigh-in, you'll know exactly what to do.

**Be prepared:** Bring a small screwdriver to remove the weight plate if you need to add more split shot during weigh-in.

**Storage:** Store your finished car in a zipper gallon-size bag before the race. This will keep your wheels clean, so they run smoothly. There are a lot of tips here that will help you keep your car wheels and axles clean—it is very important!

**Clean hands:** Make sure your hands are clean before holding your car, especially if you just ate a donut! All that sticky stuff will mess up your wheels and make your car run slower.

**Holding the car:** Don't hold your car by the wheels. Hold it by the center. You don't want to mess up all the work you just did to get the wheels rolling super-fast!

**Not a toy—yet:** Never roll your car on any surface before the race—especially the floor. Dirt will stick to your wheels and slow your car down. Wait until after the races are over before you play with your car!

**Line it up:** When you put your car on the track to race, make sure the wheels are completely in the lane and not sitting up on the lane guides. If not, your car could crash during the race.

## Round #1

| Lane Number | Lane # 1 | Lane # 2 | Lane # 3 | Lane # 4 |
|---|---|---|---|---|
| Time | | | | |
| Position | | | | |

## Round #2

| Lane Number | Lane # 1 | Lane # 2 | Lane # 3 | Lane # 4 |
|---|---|---|---|---|
| Time | | | | |
| Position | | | | |

## Round #3

| Lane Number | Lane # 1 | Lane # 2 | Lane # 3 | Lane # 4 |
|---|---|---|---|---|
| Time | | | | |
| Position | | | | |

Did you advance to the Final Round?　❑ Yes　❑ No

## Final Round

| Lane Number | Lane # 1 | Lane # 2 | Lane # 3 | Lane # 4 |
|---|---|---|---|---|
| Time | | | | |
| Position | | | | |

# MY MEMORIES

## Race Details:

My car's name: _____

Date: _____

Location: _____

Number of competitors: _____

## Race Car Details:

Car Number: _____

How long did it take to build?

_____

_____

Favorite details on my car:

_____

_____

_____

_____

Things we could improve next year:

_____

_____

_____

_____

## Finishing positions:

Race #1 _____

Race #2 _____

Race #3 _____

Race #4 _____

Race #5 _____

Race #6 _____

Race #7 _____

Race #8 _____

Finals _____

## Favorite memories:

_____

_____

_____

_____

_____

_____

Place a photo of building your car

Place a photo of building your car

Place a photo of building your car

Place a photo of your pinewood derby event

Place a photo of your pinewood derby event

Place a photo of your pinewood derby event